AN APPLE A DAY

Jeanne Voltz

Illustrated by Lorraine Epstein

Irena Chalmers Cookbooks

Published in the United States of America by
Irena Chalmers Cookbooks, Inc., 23 East 92nd St., New York, NY 10028
Sales Office: P.O. Box 988, Denton, NC 27239, (800) 334-8128

ISBN: 0-941034-35-6 E D C B A 6 5 4 3 275/25

Cover design by Milton Glaser; photograph by Matthew Klein
Book design by Mary Ann Joulwan

TABLE OF CONTENTS

INTRODUCTION

One recent autumn dusk in New York City, as lights bejeweled the skyscrapers around us, a dozen apple lovers sat in a conference room, tasting more than 20 varieties of apples. We savored the sweetness of a Red Delicious, harvested a few days earlier in an orchard in North Carolina; the snap of a Newtown Pippin; the faint perfume of a Mutsu; and the tanginess of a Granny Smith, shipped from California. The Golden Delicious fulfilled its reputation for juicy sweetness; the Summer Rambo, sweet-sour and sun-ripened, had a taste that took me straight back to childhood summers, and the daily chore of picking up apples on my grandmother's farm in Alabama. Perhaps one of her apples was a Rambo.

My grandmother's apples bore their fruit in late summer, just in time for the canning bustle that took place before school started. This meant that grandchildren, cousins, Grandmother, Mother, aunts, or anyone connected with the school system, could help. We would pour our apples into buckets of water, which sat ready to receive them when we returned from the orchard. Grandmother, Mother and my aunts would sit under the towering hickory trees peeling apples and cutting them appropriately for applesauce, apple butter, pies, cobblers and an amber-clear jelly which always smelled of apples even when it was opened months later to spread on hot biscuits with butter. I still make homemade apple jelly occasionally just for a whiff of that marvelous aroma, and I have given a recipe in this book for making it from apple trimmings. It should be just as delicious as my grandmother's if you choose fine-flavored apples.

Unfortunately, none of my grandmother's apples will ever be tasted again because, if her trees had names, I never knew them. Apples must be budded or grafted to hold their character, and the trees in her cotton patch-orchard had no names, so far as we know. But Grandma knew her apples. "Save a bucketful of apples off the tree in the north corner for pie," she would say, or "We need a bagful of apples from the tree behind the barn for applesauce." Another sort of apple was used for drying, and yet another for Brown Betty or deep-dish pie, which would be served with thick cream skimmed from the top of the milk pan.

When I grew up, and as fashions and my knowledge of food terms changed, I came to see that what we call poached apples today—faintly scented with cinnamon—are what my grandmother called stewed apples long ago. We used to have fried apples with home-smoked sausage for breakfast, but few other main-dish uses for apples occurred to us until my mother became famous for her cinnamon apple rings. She would poach them for school banquets or Exchange

Club luncheons that the missionary society catered as fund raisers, and, of course, for special dinners at home. She colored and flavored the apple rings with cinnamon red-hots, a 1930s novelty that no longer appeals to me.

Apples have connoted goodness, bounty and sweet temptation since prehistoric times, although there is some doubt whether it was actually an apple which Eve used to tempt Adam. Many authorities believe that, through the evolution of language, what turns up in the New Testament as an apple was more likely to have been a mango, a persimmon or perhaps an apricot.

Nevertheless, apples remain a sweet temptation. They are the fruit with which to bribe or honor a good teacher, the fruit that dropped from a tree and inspired Sir Isaac Newton to formulate the laws of gravity, and the fruit that William Tell was ordered by invaders to shoot from his son's head. Someone very special is called "the apple of your eye." Many a good marriage has started with the newly-wed couple planting an apple tree near the doorway of their home. And many a romance has blossomed in the shade of the old apple tree, a romantic spot in spring in an apple-growing region such as the Shenandoah Valley, when apple trees bloom and the air is rich with their sweet aroma for miles.

In this book, however, we will consider the apple principally for its gastronomic qualities. A sweetly nostalgic fruit of many faces and flavors, it is universally available, universally loved, and a food to enchant any good cook.

HISTORY

The first apples in the New World were harvested in the Massachusetts Bay Colony about 10 years after the Pilgrims' first landing, and the country has never been without apples since. Cider was the principal drink of the early colonists, and apples were its essential ingredient. In 17th-century Europe, water was rarely safe to drink because people did not know how to prevent contamination. Settlers came to the New World unaware of the many fresh streams carrying good, clear water, so they brought apple slips in order to grow apples for cider. The apple trees flourished in the New England climate, and they still do.

Apples went everywhere the white man did, and in the early 1800s John Chapman, who was born in Massachusetts, followed settlers into the Ohio Valley with his religious ministry, planting apple trees as he went. His name has gone down in history as Johny Appleseed, though most food historians think it was actual trees rather than seed that he planted so carefully and efficiently. Settlers took apples ever westward, packing seeds or tree cuttings in Conestoga wagons along with their other household goods. A few seeds and trees sailed around the Horn, also, with crews and passengers seeking the opportunities of the great West.

Currently, Washington State is the greatest producer of apples, and that industry started with a few good-luck seeds given to a captain sailing from London to the West Coast in 1820. Apples are now grown in every state except Florida, Hawaii and Alaska, with New York State, Pennsylvania, Michigan and the Shenandoah Valley in Virginia ranking just below Washington's Wenatchee Valley in production.

Today, we prize apples chiefly for fresh eating and cooking. Hard cider, a staple in Colonial times, has become a rarity, because the development of pasteurization provided a means of keeping sweet cider fresh. These days, most apples are processed as cider or apple juice, applesauce, canned pie filling or unsweetened apple slices. A small number of apples go into hard cider, applejack, jellies, jams and such novelties as canned baked apples and candies.

Apple development continues, and several commercial varieties, including the Cortland, were introduced in this century. The marketing of apples has been a revolution with the development of new storage techniques that can keep the fruit safe and sound for months. Various marketing groups have mounted sophisticated educational programs to inform the consumer of the best ways to select and use apples. They also attempt to instruct everybody in the distribution chain—packers, truckers, marketers—on how best to handle and show this versatile, long-lasting fruit.

A Puritan housewife might have laughed at her great-great-great-granddaughter's concern with choosing a good apple and keeping it snappy and fresh, but today's apple shopper would be amazed at the scarcity of apples as recently as the last century, when they were available fresh for only a short season of the year and stored for a brief time thereafter, softening and growing more wrinkled as each day passed. Today, an apple-loving child can be treated to a crisp, juicy apple virtually any time he or she wants it.

AN APPLE A DAY

Children chomping on crisp apples as they walked back to school after lunch used to prove the aphorism, "An apple a day keeps the doctor away." Don't pack that old-fashioned tale away with the myths of yesteryear! A study at Michigan State University a few years ago proved that apple eaters really *are* more healthy. For three years a group of volunteer students ate from one to three apples a day and their calls at the university health center for illnesses of any sort were compared with the number of calls made by the general university population. The apple eaters made one-third fewer calls for upper respiratory infections (colds, sore throats, coughs, and so on), they made fewer than one-sixth the calls made by the student body as a whole for tension-pressure phenomena, and fewer calls for other illnesses also.

An apple two and three-quarters inches in diameter contains about 80 calories, so an apple can be considered a slimming food when eaten instead of a higher-calorie dessert, snack or other food. Apples provide significant amounts of pectin, which is believed to aid in ridding the body of toxins and in limiting the buildup of cholesterol. The fruit is an excellent source of dietary fiber; it also provides high potassium along with a very low sodium content, and supplies modest amounts of vitamins A and C, thiamin, riboflavin and niacin.

Fresh apples are noted for preventing tooth decay, theoretically because the firm flesh is believed to have a tooth-cleaning effect—a healthy reason for packing an apple in a lunch box.

APPLES PLUS

Methods for flavoring apples vary from country to country. For example, Americans and Northern Europeans flavor apples with cinnamon, ginger, nutmeg, cloves and allspice, while French cooks use butter and vanilla. Apples may be complemented by such diverse flavorings as cardamom (try it in apple pie or applesauce), curry powder, chili

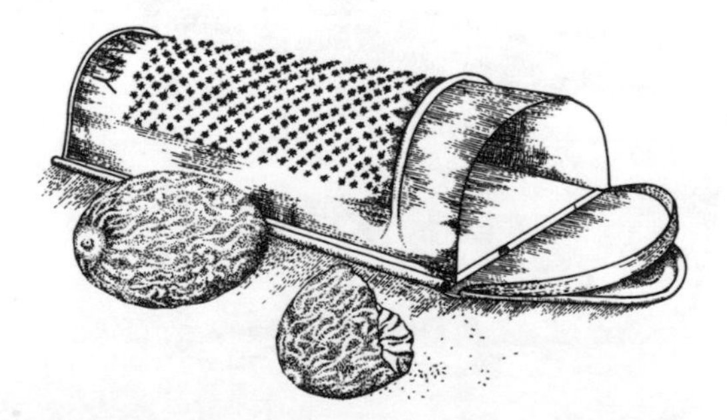

powder, horseradish, and flowery flavorings such as rose-geranium and orange-flower water.

Apples combine happily with almost any other fruit: oranges, plums, prunes, grapes, cranberries, bananas, pears, apricots or peaches. All citrus fruits taste good with apples and low-acid apples are enhanced by the peel or juice of a lemon or orange. Fruit-flavored liqueurs such as Chambord (black raspberry), Framboise (raspberry), or one of the several varieties of orange-flavored liqueur make an elegant dessert when combined with lightly poached apples. Calvados and applejack, the two great apple brandies, bourbon, rum and other spirits also go well with apples.

A flaky crust is the American ideal combination with apples in pies, cobblers and other pastries. Buttered breadcrumbs also do good things with apples in Bettys, Charlottes and other desserts.

In main dishes, apples go well with onions, winter squashes and celery for flavor perkiness. Apples are especially complementary to pork, ham and poultry—and, for novelty, a slice of apple on a thick hamburger is a treat.

The affinity of apples with cheese runs the gamut from the usual cheese, apple and bread snack combination to a slab of good cheddar on a slice of hot apple pie. The ultimate apple-cheese partnership is a full-flavored apple with a few slices of cheese for dessert. Try a Red Delicious with well-ripened Brie or Roquefort, a Winesap with fresh goat cheese or Muenster, a Jonathan with Gruyère, a Northern Spy with Bel Paese or a Golden Delicious with Camembert. A good fresh ricotta is a perfect accompaniment to fresh applesauce or poached apples with a sprinkle of cinnamon or ginger, and cottage cheese or fresh full-cream cheeses make a feast with a simple apple compote.

Californians extol good port wine, well-aged Tillamook (a cheddar from Oregon), a tangy Washington State apple and English walnuts as the epitome of a high-style dessert. Many business contracts and romances have flowered over such fare—gloriously simple and simply glorious.

TOOLS FOR PREPARING APPLES

The world's simplest way of preparing an apple is the time-honored schoolboy method of wiping an apple on shirt sleeve and biting into it. For more sophisticated uses, other tools are helpful. A good sharp knife, or a set of them, saves time and tedium. You need a good paring knife that fits your hand well for peeling, a chef's knife for dicing and a thin-bladed knife for coring. However, a sharp sturdy corer saves tedious carving around the seeds and core.

A flat sectioner (a metal disc with sturdy blades) will cut an apple into 8 to 12 segments, and removes the core when the sectioner is pushed firmly down through the apple on a cutting board. A swivel-bladed peeler can be used to peel an apple, although a good paring knife works as fast if you peel the apple in a spiral.

An apple may be sliced in a processor or on a mandoline, if you cut the apple to the size of the processor feed tube, or lay it flat against the mandoline blade.

If you bake lots of pies, do invest in at least one deep pie pan with a rim high enough to hold juices. A tart pan with a removable bottom makes quiches and some tarts easier to manage.

Saucepans and kettles coated with enamel or made of stainless steel or another good-quality material that will not react with the acid in apples are the best to use for making applesauce, poaching apples or for other stove-top dishes. Make sure that graters or other tools to be used with apples are plated with chrome or stainless steel, to avoid discoloring the fruit or the tool. Good-quality plastic graters may also be used.

VARIETIES

More than 7,000 apple varieties are named, and more than 100 of these are grown commercially in the United States. The list that follows describes the apples you are most likely to find in markets, but there are many more you might find locally. Buy and enjoy them! The chart on page 15 gives suggested uses for popular apples, but your own taste is the final word. Any apple you like is best, and the line between a good cooking apple and a good eating apple is fine indeed.

Red Delicious This apple's sweet, mild flavor makes it the Number One volume apple in the world. It is also prized for its looks—a bright red skin and a tapering shape with conspicuous knobs at the base. The first Red Delicious was found on a farm in Iowa in the 19th century. It is harvested in October and is held in refrigerated storage through the spring, but it quickly turns mealy out of refrigeration.

Golden Delicious This, the world's second most popular apple, is billed as an all-purpose apple, which is true if you allow for its sweetness and reduce the sugar when cooking with it. The first Golden Delicious tree was a chance seedling on a farm in West Virginia. It is an ideal salad apple, as it does not turn dark rapidly. The skin of a Golden Delicious is pale green or greenish-yellow and is speckled with pores, which are natural and unnoticeable on darker apples. The Golden Delicious is harvested in late September and keeps into April and May.

Granny Smith This bright green apple, unknown in this country until 1960, is the third best-seller in the world. It was originally brought from New Zealand to fill the gap in the summer when few United States apples were available; It is now grown in California and France. The name comes from Mrs. Smith who discovered the first tree growing in her yard in Australia, where the apple soon became a top favorite. Because of a fruit-fly embargo, however, no apples are shipped to the United States from Australia, so our early summer Granny Smiths are imported from New Zealand. The Granny is a cool green color, firm, tart and juicy. It is good for pies and other cooking, and tangy-apple lovers like it for fresh eating.

Lady Apple This rosy-cheeked miniature is the Pomme d'Api, believed to have been the apple of ancient Rome. It is a sweet, full-flavored dessert apple, although it is more often used for decoration than for eating. Good uncooked as well as lightly cooked, it has a short season, from October to Christmas and New Year.

Newtown Pippin The original Newtown grew from a seed in Flushing, Long Island, when it was called Newtown—a site which has long since been enveloped by New York City. The Newtown became the talk of London after Benjamin Franklin distributed samples to George III's advisers while seeking aid for the colonists. Later, Queen Victoria reputedly preferred the Newtown to any other apple on the royal table. However, the Newtown's growing requirements are so special that growers have almost abandoned it. If you find one, try it for its crisp texture and slight tanginess. It has a yellowish-green skin.

Rhode Island Greening This and the Winesap are probably the oldest named varieties in this country. Until the advent of the Granny Smith, this was one of the few green-skinned apples grown commercially. The first tree grew from a seed near Newport, Rhode Island. The fruit has a rich, tart flavor, and crisp flesh that snaps pleasantly when you bite a raw apple, and it is first class for pies, cobblers and other cooking. Its season is from October to March.

Winesap If you have never walked into a market or orchard perfumed by the heady aroma of Winesaps, you've missed an apple happening. The dark red, yellow-streaked apple is crisp and firm, and its flavor is sweetly pungent. Good for cooking as well as fresh eating, it is harvested in November and will keep in storage into May.

McIntosh Gnarled "Mac" trees growing on Vermont farms might be antiques. The first McIntosh was found on a farm in Ontario,

Canada, in the early 1800s, and Vermonters and upstate New Yorkers were planting "Macs" a few years later. The skin is green striped with red and the flesh is tender, sweet and aromatic. "Macs" are good for fresh eating and fine for applesauce and whenever you want a smooth light texture. They are harvested in September and sold into April.

Jonathan The first Jonathan grew in Kingston, New York. This apple has poor storing quality, so it is disappearing from commercial production. It has a yellow skin covered with red stripes, and firm white flesh that is tender, juicy and richly flavored, making it good for eating or cooking. It is an October apple.

Macoun This apple is a cross between the McIntosh, which it closely resembles, and the Jersey Black. It was bred in the 1920s and is considered a top-quality dessert apple. It can be cooked, too. The skin is red and the fruit richly flavored. Macouns ripen in October and will keep into the spring.

Northern Spy This variety, first grown in Ontario County, New York, is popular in New England. Large and round, with a yellow skin striped almost solidly with red, it is fragrant, slightly tart and valued for fresh eating as well as cooking. The Spy is harvested in November and under ideal storage conditions, it holds a good flavor into February.

Rome Beauty This apple sprang up as a seedling in Ohio. It is good-looking, large and deep red, sometimes with a golden cheek. An easy apple to grow, it is abundantly available despite its rather mealy flesh, and can be used either for cooking or for fresh eating.

Cortland This a a 20th-century apple, developed at the New York Agricultural Experiment Station in Geneva, New York. It is a cross between the Ben Davis, an old variety, and the McIntosh. The apple is sweet and suitable for fresh eating or cooking. The fact that its flesh stays white for a while after cutting makes it a superior apple for use in salads. The Cortland is harvested in October and keeps into December.

Gravenstein This apple from Northern Europe was brought to California in the middle of the last century and great quantities are harvested from the orchards around Sebastopol, north of San Francisco, in August and September. The Gravenstein is a slightly lopsided round apple and has a yellow skin marked with bright red. Its flesh is full-flavored and tender-crisp, and much of the crop goes into commercial applesauce and apple juice. It is also prized as an eating apple, and fresh fruit is available into November.

Stayman This apple grew as a sucker from a Winesap tree and closely resembles a Winesap. It is rich-flavored, aromatic and crisp, with a bright red skin. The Stayman is harvested in October and keeps for several months.

York Imperial This was a chance seedling found on a farm near York, Pennsylvania, in the early 1800s. The skin is mixed red and green and the flesh is crisp, juicy and fragrant. The apple is good for both cooking and eating, but most Yorks go for processing. It ripens in November and fresh apples keep into the spring.

Grimes Golden This seedling was discovered on a farm in Virginia in the 18th century. The skin is a rich yellow color and the flesh is juicy and crisp with a spicy flavor. Suitable both for cooking and for fresh eating, it is harvested in September and does not keep well.

Ida Red This is a new variety that you might see at farm stands in any apple-growing region. It is red-skinned and its firm, tart flesh and sweet aroma make it good for both eating and cooking.

Empire This is another newcomer, a cross between two favorites, the McIntosh and the Red Delicious, with some of the firm, juicy texture of a "Mac" and the sweet perfume of a Delicious. It is harvested in September and keeps well.

Mutsu A variety bred in Japan which is yellow-skinned and tender with a pleasantly fragrant flavor.

Summer Rambo An oldie, said to be Johnny Appleseed's favorite, this is considered to be primarily a cooking apple.

Baldwin The most popular apple in the Northeast in the 1800s. Baldwin trees can still be bought, however, and if you find an apple, it is good for cooking or fresh eating.

Roxbury Russet This very old variety has fine fresh eating and cooking qualities, but its skin has the rough, slightly spotted look characteristic of a Russet. In consequence it has lost out to prettier apples, in spite of its juicy flesh and lively flavor.

Twenty Ounce This apple weighs 20 ounces or more per fruit, the size of a cantaloupe, but it is very rare now. In order to prepare it, the whole apple would be baked, the core and seeds scooped out and the center filled with maple syrup for a family dessert.

KNOW YOUR APPLES

October is the traditional apple month because it is then that the largest supplies of fresh, firm and flavorful apples are in the markets. However, you may expect to find good apples from late July or early August into May or June the following year, when well-kept apples come out of storage for off-season use. Generally, apples are crisper and tangier early in the season.

I have compiled this guide to apple uses from the opinions of food experts and industry specialists along with my own love of the fruit. But, as always, your own taste will be your best guide to a good apple for your table and fruit bowl.

Variety & Region	*Eating*	*Baking*	*Applesauce*	*Pies & Tarts*
Red Delicious Worldwide	X		X	
Golden Delicious Worldwide	X	X	X	X
Granny Smith Nationwide New Zealand, France, California (now growing)		X	X	X
Gravenstein California				X
Jonathan Great Lakes Area	X	X	X	X
Rome Beauty East, Midwest	X	X	X	X
McIntosh East, Midwest	X	X	X	X
Macoun East, Northeast	X	X	X	X
Northern Spy Northeast		X	X	X
Winesap East, Northeast, Washington State	X	X	X	X

APPLES WITH MEATS

Meat and poultry cooked with apples take on a welcome tang and a lightening of textures. These fresh ideas fit numerous meal situations, from snacks to large holiday dinners.

RHODE ISLAND POT ROAST

Snappy fall apples such as Rhode Island Greenings, Jonathans or Northern Spys mellow the flavor of an old-fashioned pot roast.

Serves 8

3- to 4-pound beef blade pot roast
¼ cup flour
1 teaspoon salt
¼ teaspoon pepper
2 medium-size onions, sliced
½ cup water, beef broth or apple juice
1 acorn squash or piece large winter squash (about 1 pound)
2 tart apples, cored and quartered

Trim the surface fat from the roast and fry it in a large skillet. Mix the flour, salt and pepper together and rub all over the meat. Brown the meat in the fat, turning to brown on all sides. Pour off the excess drippings. Add the onions and cook until they are tender but not browned. Add the water or broth. Cover and simmer for 2 hours.

Peel the squash and scrape off any seeds and stringy pulp. Slice or cube the squash and add it to the pot roast along with the apples. Cover and simmer for 30 to 35 minutes longer or until the meat and vegetables are tender.

CURRIED LAMB WITH APPLE

A marvelous dish for dealing with leftover roast lamb, in which apple takes the place of the more exotic fruits traditionally served with curry.

Serves 4

2 tablespoons butter
1 medium-size onion, chopped
1 tart juicy apple, cored and chopped
2 cloves garlic, minced
1½-2 cups cubed roast lamb, visible fat removed
1 tablespoon curry powder, or to taste
1 teaspoon salt
2 tablespoons flour
1-1½ cups chicken or beef broth
Freshly cooked rice
Curry condiments, to taste

Heat the butter in a large saucepan. Add the onion, apple and garlic. Cook, stirring occasionally, until the onion is tender but not browned. Add the lamb, mix well, then stir in the curry powder, salt and flour. Cook and stir for about 30 seconds. Add 1 cup of the broth and cook and stir until the sauce is smooth and thickened.

If the sauce is too thick, add more broth to taste and cook and stir until it is well blended. Serve hot with rice and such accompaniments as chutney, chopped peanuts, onion, banana slices, chopped egg and bacon.

PORK CHOPS WITH APPLES AND MADEIRA

A colorful vegetable such as sweet potatoes (baked and split to show their brilliance) or brussels sprouts will brighten the plate and taste good with these richly flavored chops.

Serves 4

4 thin pork chops
Flour, salt and pepper, as needed
2 apples, cored and cut in rings
2-3 tablespoons Madeira or cream sherry
¾ cup light or heavy cream

Trim the fat from the edges of the chops and fry it until crisp in a heavy skillet. Coat the chops lightly with flour and brown them in the fat, turning once. Season with salt and pepper after turning. When they are browned on both sides, remove them to a warm platter.

Cook the apples in a single layer in the pan drippings until they are lightly browned. Transfer to the platter with the chops.

Add the Madeira to the pan drippings and bring to a brisk boil. Stir in the cream and heat through, but do not boil. Pour the sauce over the chops and apples, and serve hot.

CIDER-BRAISED HAM

This simple embellishment is perfect when plain ham isn't quite enough. It is good with a boneless smoked shoulder butt, too.

Serves 4

2½-3 pounds boneless fully cooked ham, in 1 piece
About 3 cups apple juice
3 2-inch cinnamon sticks, broken
6-8 whole cloves
3 firm apples, peeled, cored and sliced

Place the ham in a deep skillet with a domed lid, a large deep saucepan or a Dutch oven. Add apple juice to a depth of about 2 inches. Add the cinnamon and cloves. Cover and simmer for 1½ to 2 hours, until the flavor of the ham is fully developed. Remove the spices with a slotted spoon and pour off all but about ½ inch of the apple-juice broth. Add the apples and simmer until they are just tender.

Place the ham in the center of a platter; carve and fan out the slices for an attractive presentation. Arrange the apples around the ham. Serve with mustard, if you wish.

FRIED HAM WITH APPLES

Any ham treated this way is excellent fare, but country ham with apples is fit for the gods.

Serves 4

4 thin slices Smithfield or other dry-cured ham, or a ½-inch-thick slice moist-cured ham
2 apples, peeled, cored and sliced
1-2 teaspoons sugar

Warm a heavy skillet over moderate heat and rub with the edges of the ham pieces to coat it with fat. Place the ham in the skillet and cook over medium-high heat until browned. Turn and brown the other side. Remove to a warm platter.

Pour off all but about 1 tablespoon of ham fat. Add the apples, and cook and stir gently until they are lightly browned and tender but not mushy. Sprinkle with sugar and serve hot with the ham. Hot biscuits and grits are fine accompaniments.

SAUSAGE APPLE LOAF

This peppery-flavored loaf is as good cold as it is hot.

Serves 8
Preheat the oven to 350 degrees

1 cup fine dry breadcrumbs
1 cup diced apple, peeled and cored
1½ cups water
2 eggs
1 medium-size onion, chopped
1 pound lean hot pork sausage meat
1 pound leanest ground beef

Combine the breadcrumbs, apple, water, eggs and onion. Add the sausage meat and mix it in well with a sturdy spoon or fork. Add the beef and mix it in well. Pack the mixture into a 5-by-9-inch loaf pan. Bake in the preheated oven for 1 hour, or until the juices run clear when a thin-bladed knife is inserted into the center of the loaf. Let stand for 10 minutes, then drain off the excess fat and turn the meat loaf out onto a warm platter.

BACON-APPLE BITES

These savory tidbits go fast at a party. They fill out a luncheon or brunch platter, too, as a side dish for eggs or hot breads.

Makes 16 pieces
Preheat the oven to 400 degrees

½ pound bacon
2 apples, cored and cut in eighths

Arrange the bacon on a rack in a broiler pan. Bake (do not broil, to avoid having to watch it constantly) for 5 minutes, so that the bacon is partially cooked but not crisp. Cut each slice of bacon crosswise with scissors. Wrap a half slice of bacon loosely around each apple chunk and secure with a wooden toothpick.

Place the wrapped apple pieces on the broiler rack and bake again for 10 to 12 minutes, until the apples are tender and the bacon is crisp. Turn as needed to cook evenly.

ROAST CHICKEN NORMANDY

This preparation for chicken is adapted from a specialty of Normandy, where cream, butter and apple brandy are plentiful.

Serves 4
Preheat the oven to 400 degrees

2 tablespoons butter
2½- to 3-pound broiler/fryer chicken
Salt and pepper to taste
¼ cup Calvados or applejack
2 tablespoons chopped onion
1 tablespoon minced parsley
2 tart apples, peeled, cored and cut in rings
¼ cup apple cider
½ cup heavy cream

Heat the butter in a large heavy skillet or in a shallow baking pan in the oven while it is preheating. Season the chicken inside and out with salt and pepper, place it on its side in the skillet or pan, and brush it with the butter. Roast for 15 minutes in the hot oven, then turn it on its other side and roast for 15 minutes longer. Remove the bird from the oven.

Turn the chicken breast up, pour the Calvados around it and ignite. When the flame dies, sprinkle the onion and parsley into the pan. Dip the apple rings in the pan drippings and arrange them around the chicken. Roast for about 30 minutes, basting once or twice with the pan drippings, until the chicken is tender and the juices run clear when the inside thigh muscle is pierced with a fork. Transfer the chicken and apples to a warm platter.

Place the skillet over moderate heat, add the cider and bring to a boil. Carefully stir in the cream, bring to a boil and simmer until slightly thickened. Carve the chicken and serve the sauce on the side.

ROAST GOOSE WITH APPLE-WALNUT STUFFING

This is the ultimate holiday bird, and the stuffing is good with chicken, turkey or duckling.

Serves 8 (with leftovers)
Preheat the oven to 325 degrees

An 8-to 10-pound goose, thawed, if frozen

Stuffing:
6 cups dry bread cubes (see below; I like to use half cornbread or whole-wheat bread)
1 large onion, chopped
2 stalks celery with leaves, chopped
4 tablespoons butter, oil or rendered goose fat
1½ teaspoons salt
¼ teaspoon pepper
1 tablespoon rubbed sage
4 tart apples, peeled, cored and chopped

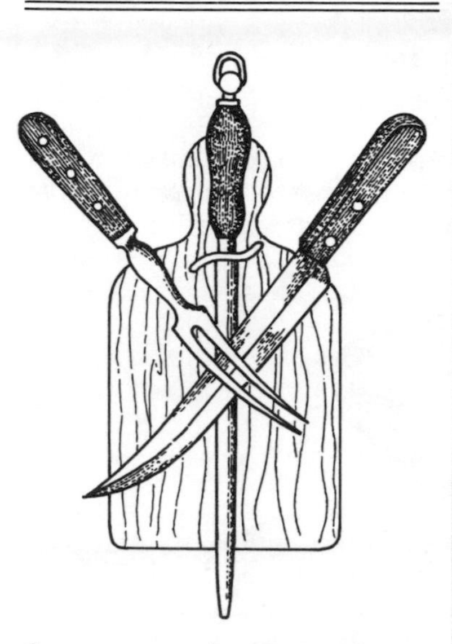

1 cup coarsely chopped walnuts
1½ cups hot poultry broth or water, or as needed

Remove any pinfeathers from the goose, using tweezers or a strawberry huller. Wipe the bird inside and out with paper towels and stuff the body cavities with paper towels to absorb any moisture. Let stand while you make the stuffing.

To prepare the bread, stack several slices and cut checkerboard fashion to cube. Spread the cubes in a shallow pan and bake in the preheated oven until they are dry and slightly crisp, about 15 minutes. Meanwhile, put the butter in a large skillet, add the onion and celery, and cook until the vegetables are tender but not browned.

Put the bread cubes in a large bowl, add the onion mixture, salt and pepper to taste, sage, apples and walnuts. Mix lightly. Add the hot broth to moisten as desired. (If the stuffing holds its shape when pressed in a mound on a spoon, it will roast moist but not pasty inside the goose.)

Remove the paper towels and pat the bird dry again. Spoon the stuffing lightly into the neck and body cavities. (Do not fill too full—any extra stuffing can be baked in a well-greased casserole, refrigerated to bake within a day or two, or frozen for later use with another bird.) Truss the goose, using kitchen twine and skewers, and place, breast up, on a rack in a shallow roasting pan. If the tail juts over the rim of the pan, wrap it in foil shaped to divert the drippings back into the pan. Prick the skin of the goose in several places to allow the fat to cook out as the bird roasts.

Roast in the preheated oven for 3 to 3½ hours, until a meat thermometer inserted in the thickest part of the inside thigh registers 185 degrees. Remove the fat from the pan with a bulb baster or spoon every 15 to 20 minutes. (Goose fat should be strained and refrigerated for use in cooking later on.)

Remove the bird to a warm platter and let it stand for 20 to 30 minutes before carving. Serve with a gravy made from the pan drippings, if desired.

APPLES AS VEGETABLES, WITH VEGETABLES AND AS SALADS

Applesauce is the conventional accompaniment to pork roast. It is also featured as part of the goose dinner in Dickens's *A Christmas Carol*. This small collection gives you a sampling of many other ways to use apples to good advantage in side dishes.

APPLESAUCE

Serves 4

1½ pounds apples (choose your favorite kind)
1 cup water, apple juice, orange juice or ginger ale
Flavoring(s) (optional): cinnamon, nutmeg, cloves, ginger, salt, pepper, chili pepper, sugar, honey, molasses, applejack, Calvados, vanilla, or other flavorings to suit the apples you have selected

Peel, core and cut up the apples. Put them in a saucepan with the liquid, cover, and boil for 15 to 20 minutes, or until the fruit is very tender and most of the liquid has been absorbed. Mash the apples with the back of a wooden spoon or a potato masher, or puree them in a blender—but be careful not to liquefy them. Sweeten and flavor to taste.

Note: You can also cook the apples unpeeled and puree the applesauce in a food mill.

POACHED LADY APPLES

These decorative apple miniatures will keep several weeks in their syrup, if stored in covered containers in the refrigerator. Serve them as a garnish for meats, or as a dessert.

Makes 12

12 lady apples, preferably with stems on
1 cup water
½ cup sugar
1 slice lemon

Wash the apples and pick off any wilted leaves. It is difficult to core lady apples because they are so small, so I slash them deeply at the bud end, making a cross, to help the syrup penetrate.

Bring the water, sugar and lemon to a boil in a medium-sized saucepan, stirring until the sugar has dissolved. Add the apples and simmer gently about 5 minutes, or until they are tender when pierced with a fork or the tip of a knife. Remove the apples with a slotted spoon and continue to boil the syrup until it has slightly thickened. Pour it over the apples, cover, and refrigerate.

BUTTERED APPLES AND ONIONS

An innovative restaurateur in New York serves this as a side dish with grilled calves' liver.

Serves 4

3 tablespoons butter
2 onions, peeled and sliced
4 medium-size firm apples, cored and sliced
Salt and freshly ground pepper, to taste
½ teaspoon freshly squeezed lemon juice

Heat the butter in a large skillet. Add the onions and apples, and cook, turning with a spatula occasionally, until the apples and onions are tender. Season to taste with salt and pepper. Stir in the lemon juice. Serve hot with pork chops, hamburgers or grilled liver.

APPLE-ONION SAUCE

This fruity side dish makes roast pork or any bird special.

Serves 4

2 tablespoons butter
1 large onion, peeled and sliced
3 apples (1 pound), peeled, cored and sliced
6-8 prunes, snipped in quarters
½ teaspoon cinnamon
¼ teaspoon ginger
¼ teaspoon salt
¼ cup applejack or apple juice
1 tablespoon cider vinegar

Heat the butter in a medium-sized saucepan. Add the onion and cook until it is tender but not browned. Add the apples, prunes, cinnamon, ginger and salt. Mix well and add the applejack. Cover and simmer for 20 to 30 minutes, until the apples are tender but not mushy. Add the vinegar, stir well and cook a minute or two longer.

Serve hot.

AMBER APPLE SALAD

Dressed with whipped cream instead of mayonnaise, this salad can also serve as a light dessert.

Serves 4

½ cup cold water
1 envelope unflavored gelatin
¼ cup sugar
2 tablespoons freshly squeezed lemon juice
1 cup apple juice or clear cider
1 medium-size apple (Winesap or Red Delicious)
¼ cup chopped pecans
Garnish: Leaves of curly endive or other greens
Mayonnaise

Put the water in a small saucepan and sprinkle in the gelatin. When it is thoroughly moistened, place the pan over low heat and stir until the gelatin has dissolved. Stir in the sugar and when it has dissolved, stir in the lemon juice and apple juice.

Remove from the heat and chill until the mixture is as thick as unbeaten egg white. Core, but do not peel the apple, and cut it in small cubes into the gelatin. Add the nuts and fold together. Turn the mixture into a 3-cup mold that has been rinsed in cold water and chill until set.

Unmold onto a platter, garnish with greens and serve with mayonnaise, preferably homemade, on the side.

WINTER SQUASH WITH APPLE

Butternut, buttercup or acorn squash make individual servings when halved. Large winter varieties of squash can be cubed and steamed along with the apple, seasonings and a little water.

Serves 4
Preheat the oven to 375 degrees

2 butternut, buttercup or acorn squash
2 large tart apples, cored and sliced
½ onion, chopped
Cinnamon, salt and pepper to taste
1 teaspoon sugar
2 teaspoons butter

Cut the squash in half and scoop out the seeds. Place them, cut sides down, in a greased shallow baking dish and pour in hot water to a depth of ½ inch. Bake in the preheated oven until partly tender, about 20 minutes for butternut or buttercup squash, 30 to 45 minutes for acorn squash.

Turn the squash cut sides up. Arrange a quarter of the apple slices and some of the onion in the cup of each squash half and sprinkle lightly with cinnamon, salt and pepper, to taste. Sprinkle ¼ teaspoon of the sugar over each half and dot with ½ teaspoon butter. Top up the hot water level in the dish, if necessary, to make up the depth of ½ inch again. Return to the oven and bake for 20 to 30 minutes longer, until both the squash and the apple are tender.

APPLE BEET RELISH WITH HORSERADISH

This relish-salad is an ideal complement for baked ham or roast beef.

Serves 6-8

½ cup cold water
1 envelope unflavored gelatin
¼ cup sugar
¼ cup cider vinegar
¾ cup beet juice
1 cup finely diced cooked beets, well drained
1 cup finely diced apples, cored and peeled
2-3 tablespoons prepared horseradish
Garnish (optional): Leaves of lettuce or other greens, apple slices dipped in lemon juice to preserve their color

Put the water in a small saucepan and sprinkle in the gelatin. When it is thoroughly moistened, place the pan over low heat and stir until the gelatin has dissolved. Stir in the sugar and vinegar, and when the sugar has dissolved, stir in the beet juice.

Remove from the heat and chill until the mixture is as thick as unbeaten egg white. Fold in the diced beets and apples and the horseradish. Turn into a 3- to 4-cup mold that has been rinsed in cold water, and chill until firm. Unmold onto a platter and garnish with lettuce leaves and apple slices.

WILTED GREENS WITH CHICKEN LIVERS AND APPLES

Serves 4

2 cups coarsely shredded spinach, leaf or Boston lettuce
¼ pound (4 small) chicken livers
2 tablespoons oil
1 shallot, finely chopped
1 firm tart apple, peeled, cored and sliced
2 tablespoons vinegar
2 tablespoons applejack or apple juice
Salt and pepper to taste

Place the greens in a bowl. Cut the chicken livers into small pieces, using kitchen shears. Heat the oil in a skillet, add the shallot and cook until it is tender but not browned. Add the apple and cook, turning until the slices are tinged with brown. Add the chicken livers and cook until they are lightly browned.

Add the vinegar and applejack. Heat the mixture to bubbling, pour over the greens and toss the salad immediately to wilt the greens. Season with salt and pepper to taste, and serve.

SAUERKRAUT WITH APPLES AND TOMATO

This combination makes a tangy accompaniment to frankfurters, baked spareribs and other meats.

Serves 4

1 pound sauerkraut
2 tablespoons butter or bacon drippings
1 cup chopped peeled tomatoes or 8-ounce can tomatoes, drained
2 tart apples, peeled, cored and sliced

Put the sauerkraut in a strainer or colander, drain well, run cold water through it and drain again. Heat the butter in a large skillet or medium-sized saucepan. Add the sauerkraut, tomatoes and apples. Cover and simmer for 20 minutes, stirring once or twice. Uncover and boil rapidly to reduce any excess liquid.

Serve hot.

RED CABBAGE WITH CHESTNUTS AND APPLES

This delicately spiced preparation makes a grand appearance with holiday food or game.

Serves 4-6

2 ounces salt pork or bacon, diced
2 tablespoons goose or pork drippings, or butter
1 small carrot, thinly sliced
1 medium-size onion, thinly sliced
1½ pounds red cabbage, coarsely shredded
2 large tart apples (Greening, Newtown, Granny Smith), cored and diced
2 cloves garlic, minced
1 small bay leaf, crumbled
¼ teaspoon allspice
Salt and freshly ground pepper, to taste
1 cup dry red wine or ½ cup ruby port
1 cup beef broth
12 peeled fresh or rehydrated dry chestnuts

Rinse the salt pork in hot water and dry it on paper towels. Heat the drippings or butter in a large enamelware, stainless steel or other nonmetallic saucepan. Add the salt pork, carrot and onion and cook, covered, until the onion is tender but not browned. Add the cabbage, mix well, cover and simmer for 5 minutes. Add the apples, garlic, bay leaf, allspice and salt and pepper to taste. Stir well, then add the wine and broth. Cover, bring to a boil, turn the heat low and simmer for 20 minutes. Add the chestnuts, cover and simmer for 30 minutes more, until the cabbage and chestnuts are tender.

If excess liquid remains, cook rapidly, uncovered, stirring occasionally, until most of the liquid has evaporated but the cabbage is still moist. Serve hot.

Note: To peel the chestnuts, cut a thin slice off the skin on the flat side. Put the chestnuts in a pan, cover with boiling water and simmer for 5 minutes. Remove from the heat and let stand until they are cool enough to handle. Peel off the skin, then remove the inner brown husk with a sharp knife. Return any reluctant chestnuts to the boiling water for a few minutes to facilitate peeling.

COLESLAW WITH APPLES

A refreshing change from sharp sweet-sour coleslaws, this version goes gracefully with sandwiches or cold meats.

Serves 4

½ cup mayonnaise
¼ cup apple juice
1 tablespoon cider vinegar
1 Golden or Red Delicious apple
1-1½ pounds cabbage, shredded
1 small onion, finely chopped
Salt and freshly ground pepper, to taste

Combine the mayonnaise, apple juice and vinegar in a salad bowl. Core, but do not peel the apple, and dice it into the dressing. Add the cabbage, onion and salt and pepper to taste, and toss thoroughly. Cover and refrigerate for 2 hours or longer. Mix again before serving and drain off any excess dressing.

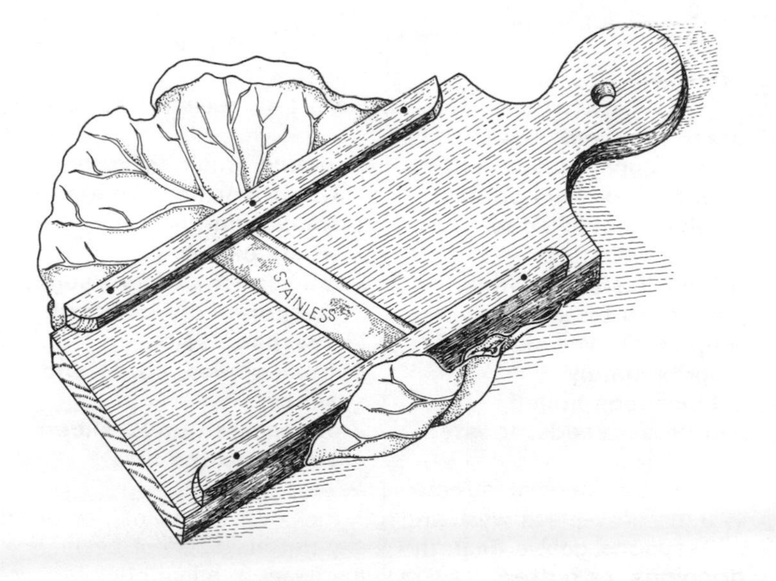

RADICCHIO AND APPLE SALAD

I discovered radicchio one December while buying take-along lunches on a drive through Germany and France. It looks like a miniature red cabbage, but resembles lettuce in both taste and texture, features that make it a striking, tender and fresh-flavored addition to a salad or sandwich. Imported radicchio commands stiff prices, but the seeds are offered by specialty seed companies, and a tiny garden plot grows enough for a family. Radicchio and Golden Delicious apples make a stunning salad.

If you like, you can make a red apple counterpart using McIntosh or Red Delicious apples contrasted with Belgian endive, watercress or Bibb lettuce and shreds of crispy iceberg.

Serves 4

1 small head radicchio
1 small bunch red-leaf lettuce
2 Golden Delicious apples
1½ tablespoons red wine vinegar
Salt and freshly ground pepper to taste
½ cup sunflower oil, approximately
2 tablespoons hulled sunflower seeds, toasted

Carefully separate the radicchio and lettuce leaves and wash and dry them thoroughly. Tear the leaves into a salad bowl, leaving the tiniest radicchio leaves whole. Chill until just before serving.

Wash, dry and core the apples, but do not peel. Cut into cubes, then add to the salad in the bowl. Sprinkle in the vinegar and toss lightly. Sprinkle with salt, pepper and about 2 tablespoons of the oil. Toss again, adding just enough more oil to coat the salad thoroughly. Top with the sunflower seeds, toss well and serve as a first course, as a side dish to the main course, or as a luncheon entree along with well-ripened Brie or goat cheese and good French bread.

BAKED BEANS WITH APPLES

Apples lighten the texture and flavor of this stout-hearted American classic.

Serves 4
Preheat the oven to 325 degrees

½ pound small white or Great Northern beans
1 small onion
2 whole cloves
2 tablespoons brown sugar
2 teaspoons dry mustard
½ teaspoon salt
3 small apples, cored and sliced
2 ounces salt pork, sliced almost to the rind

Pick over the beans, removing any grit or imperfect beans. Put the beans in a large bowl, cover

generously with water and soak overnight. Drain off and discard the water, then put the beans in a large saucepan and add fresh water to a height of 2 inches above the beans. Cover, and simmer until the beans are tender, about 1 hour. Drain, reserving the liquid.

Peel the onion, leaving it whole, and stud with the cloves. Thoroughly grease a lidded bean pot or deep casserole and add the beans to it in alternate layers with the brown sugar, mustard, salt and sliced apples. Bury the clove-studded onion near the center and push the salt pork, rind uppermost, into the beans at the top. Add enough reserved bean liquid or hot water to cover the beans. Cover the pot and bake in the preheated oven for 3 hours, or until the beans are very tender. Add more bean liquid or water as needed to keep the top moist. Serve hot.

CHEESE GRITS WITH APPLE

Sunday lunch or brunch is grand indeed when you serve this version of an old favorite along with baked ham or chicken.

Serves 8
Preheat the oven to 325 degrees

2 cups water
½ cup grits
½ teaspoon salt
2 tablespoons butter
1½-2 cups shredded sharp cheddar cheese
1 egg
¼ cup milk
2 red-skinned apples, cored and cut in wedges

Bring the water to a boil, and stir in the grits and salt. Cover and cook until the grits are tender and the water is absorbed, about 5 minutes for quick-cooking grits. Stir in the butter, all but ½ cup of the cheese, the egg and the milk. Combine well, then turn into a well-greased 9-by-13-inch baking dish. Cover with foil and bake in the preheated oven for 40 minutes.

Remove from the oven, sprinkle with the remaining cheese, and arrange the apple wedges in rows over the top of the grits, pressing in lightly. Bake, uncovered, for 20 minutes longer, or until the grits mixture is firm and the apples tender. Let stand for 15 to 20 minutes before serving. The grits should be warm.

DESSERTS, DESSERTS

Apples have been appreciated for their dessert qualities for centuries. These selections update a few old favorites and suggest some new ideas for enjoying apples as a sweet course.

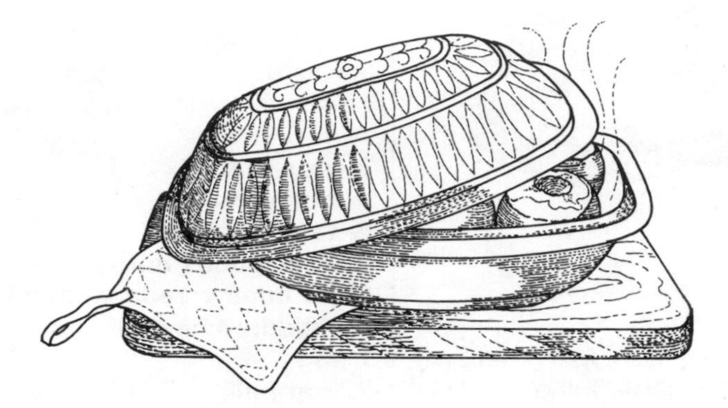

CLAY-POT BAKED APPLES WITH CHEESE

Apples baked in a clay pot have an aroma that is unbeatable. If you have not yet acquired one of these popular cooking utensils, you can use a regular casserole lined and covered with aluminum foil.

Serves 6
Preheat the oven to 450 degrees

6 apples
3 tablespoons brown sugar
Cinnamon, to taste
6 2-inch squares sharp cheddar cheese

Soak a clay baking pot in cold water to cover for 15 to 20 minutes. Place a sheet of aluminum foil or cooking parchment loosely in the bottom.

Core the apples, and peel them about halfway down from the top. Arrange them on the foil in the pot. Fill the cavities with the brown sugar and sprinkle each apple lightly with cinnamon. Cover the pot and bake in the preheated oven for 30 minutes, or until the apples are tender.

Remove from the oven and remove the cover carefully to avoid burning yourself with steam. Place a square of cheese on each apple and return the pot to the oven for a minute or two. Serve warm as an accompaniment to a meat dish, or as a dessert on its own.

APPLE BROWN BETTY

As one of the tests for my Girl Scout merit badge in cookery, I had to bake Brown Betty buried in a hole heated with coals. I recall that the apple was crunchy and that there were a few crumbs of dirt in the Betty, but I thought it was luscious. Baked in a reliable oven it is an enduring family favorite.

Serves 4
Preheat the oven to 375 degrees

3 cups small bread cubes (raisin bread is nice)
3-4 tablespoons butter, melted
½ teaspoon cinnamon
Dash nutmeg
⅔ cup dark brown sugar, firmly packed
4 cups peeled and chopped tart apples

Combine the bread cubes, butter, cinnamon, nutmeg and sugar. Layer the apples and the bread-cube mixture into a well greased 5- to 6-cup baking dish. Cover and bake for 30 minutes. Remove the cover and bake for 30 minutes longer, or until the apples are tender and the top is golden brown. Serve warm with milk, cream or ice cream.

OZARK PUDDING

This crunchy torte-like pudding has other names: Mrs. Truman's Pudding (so-called when the late Harry Truman was President and the White House circulated a version of this as a favorite recipe) and Huguenot Torte (after the Huguenots who settled in the Carolina low country and served this thrifty but delectable fare). I don't know how it got the name given here—do you?

Serves 4
Preheat the oven to 325 degrees

1 egg
⅔ cup sugar
2 tablespoons flour
1½ teaspoons baking powder
1 teaspoon vanilla
½ cup peeled and diced firm apples
1 teaspoon freshly squeezed lemon juice (if the apples are sweet)
½ cup chopped pecans

Beat the egg with the sugar until the sugar has dissolved. Stir in the flour, baking powder, vanilla, diced apple, lemon juice and pecans. Turn the mixture into a well-greased 9-inch pie pan. Bake in the preheated oven for 35 minutes, or until the top is firm and lightly browned.

Serve warm in dessert bowls with cream or softened ice cream, if desired.

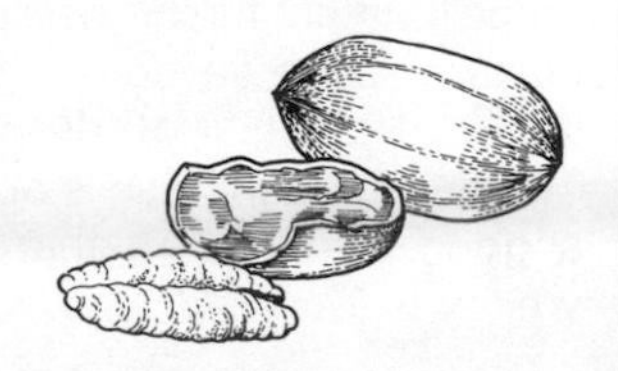

POACHED APPLES AND QUINCE

My great-grandmother kept a quince tree in her orchard for such pleasures as this—a fruit dish for dessert or breakfast.

Serves 4

1 quince
4 cups water
2 teaspoons freshly squeezed lemon juice
1 pound apples, peeled and sliced
2 cups sugar

Wash, peel and core the quince. Put the trimmings in a saucepan with the water, bring to a boil and boil, uncovered, until the water becomes slightly syrupy. Skim out the trimmings.

Slice the quince and add to the liquid with the lemon juice, apples and sugar. Heat and stir until the sugar has dissolved. Boil gently, uncovered, until the apples and the quince are tender. Serve at room temperature with cream or ice cream, if desired.

APPLE CHARLOTTE

Soft-whipped cream is the classic embellishment for this dessert, but custard sauce flavored with Calvados also sets it off deliciously. The best bread to use is one with a good, firm crumb that toasts well.

Serves 4-6
Preheat the oven to 350 degrees

8 tablespoons butter
2½ pounds (8-9 medium-size) apples, peeled, cored, and thinly sliced
¼-⅓ cup sugar
2 tablespoons Calvados or applejack
1 teaspoon vanilla
7-8 slices firm bread (preferably homemade)

Heat 1 tablespoon of the butter in a large saucepan. Add the apples and cook over low heat for about 10 minutes, stirring often, until they form a thick, almost smooth paste. (If the filling is too thin, the charlotte will not hold its shape when unmolded.) Flavor the apples with the Calvados and vanilla.

Meanwhile, trim the crusts from the bread and cut it into squares and fingers. You will need enough to completely line a 4- to 5-cup charlotte mold or straight-sided baking pan. Melt the remaining butter in a medium-sized skillet and dip the bread pieces into it. Place a slice of bread in the bottom of the mold and fill in with strips, overlapping as needed, to make a solid layer. Line the sides with more strips, overlapping them slightly. Pack the apple filling firmly into the bread case. Mound the filling slightly in the center. Top with 3 or 4 half slices of bread dipped in butter.

Bake in the preheated oven for

30 to 45 minutes, until the top and sides are golden. Remove the charlotte from the oven and let it cool in the mold for 15 to 20 minutes, then invert the pudding carefully onto a serving platter.

Serve warm or at room temperature with softly whipped cream or a custard sauce.

APPLE MOUSSE

This version of apple snow is a summery treat to make when the early apples, Newtown Pippins and Greenings, come in. Later, when apples become less sharp and tasty, reduce the sugar to 1/3 cup.

Serves 6-8

2 tablespoons butter
¼ cup applejack or apple juice
2 pounds (6-7 cups) tart apples, peeled, cored and chopped
1 envelope unflavored gelatin
2 tablespoons cold water
½ cup brown sugar, firmly packed
1 teaspoon freshly squeezed lemon juice
1 cup heavy cream, whipped to soft peaks
Toasted chopped pecans or shredded coconut, for decoration

Heat the butter in a medium-sized heavy saucepan. Add the applejack and apples. Bring to a boil, turn the heat to low, then cover and cook for 20 to 30 minutes, until the apples are very soft. Stir occasionally while the mixture is cooking to break up the apple pieces. Beat with a sturdy spoon or mixer to make a slightly chunky sauce.

Meanwhile, soften the gelatin in the cold water. Beat the gelatin and the brown sugar into the hot applesauce. Cool to room temperature, then fold in the lemon juice and whipped cream. Pile the mixture into dessert bowls and chill for 2 to 3 hours. Sprinkle heavily with pecans or coconut before serving.

APPLE-CRANBERRY CRISP

Serve this on the day after Thanksgiving, when there is some cranberry sauce left over from the holiday feast.

Serves 4
Preheat the oven to 375 degrees

2 tablespoons butter
2-4 tablespoons brown sugar
2 tablespoons rolled oats
2 tablespoons flour
3 apples, peeled, cored and cubed
¼ cup whole cranberry sauce

Blend the butter with the sugar, oats and flour, using your fingers or the back of a spoon. Put the apples into a greased shallow 1-quart baking dish. Stir in the cranberry sauce and coat the apples well. Sprinkle the oat mixture over the top.

Bake in the preheated oven for 30 minutes, or until the apples are tender and the topping is bubbly and lightly browned. Serve warm or cold.

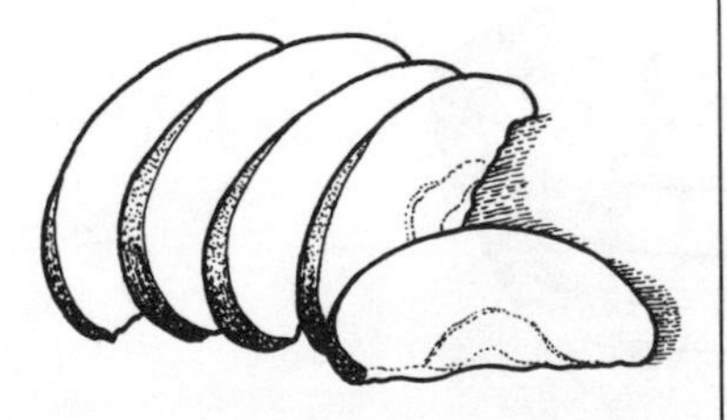

OVEN PANCAKE WITH APPLES

Serve this with lemon wedges and sugar as a simple dessert, or with bacon and eggs for an easy supper or quick luncheon.

Serves 4
Preheat the oven to 425 degrees

3 tablespoons butter
2 eggs
½ cup milk
¼ teaspoon salt
½ cup flour
1 large or 2 small apples, peeled, cored, and sliced
Juice of ½ lemon
Confectioners' sugar, if desired, for decoration

Put the butter in an 8-inch-square baking pan to melt while you are preheating the oven. Meanhile, beat the eggs until they are foamy. Beat in the milk, salt and flour and continue beating until the mixture is completely smooth. Take the baking pan from the oven, spread the sliced apples in the hot butter, and top with the batter. Bake in the oven for 30 minutes, or until puffed and golden.

Remove the pancake from the oven, squeeze lemon juice over the top and sprinkle with confectioners' sugar, if desired. Serve immediately—the pancake will fall as it cools.

BOURBON-APPLE OMELETTE

This makes a stylish dessert for two, and you will find additional ways of showing off the sauce—in crêpes, on soufflés or with other desserts.

Serves 2

Sauce:
2 tablespoons butter
2 apples, peeled, cored, and thinly sliced
1-2 tablespoons sugar
¼ cup bourbon

Omelettes:
4 eggs
2 tablespoons water
½ teaspoon sugar
1-2 tablespoons butter

To prepare the sauce, heat the butter in a medium-sized skillet. Add the apples and cook until they are tender and tinged with gold. Sprinkle with the sugar and turn the apples once or twice to brown lightly. Stir in the bourbon, bring to a brisk boil and remove from the heat. Keep hot while you make the omelettes.

To prepare the omelettes, beat the eggs with a fork or spoon until they are well blended but not foamy. Beat in the water and sugar.

Heat an omelette pan (or heavy skillet with a nonstick coating) until a drop of water sizzles in it for a few seconds and evaporates. Heat 1 tablespoon of the butter, being careful not to let it brown. Pour in half the egg mixture. Slide the pan over moderate heat to set the omelette and keep it moving freely in the pan. With a fork, pull the cooked edges to the center, then tilt the pan and let the uncooked egg run to the edges.

At the stage when the omelette has set on the bottom but is still moist in the center, spoon in 2 or 3 pieces of hot apple from the sauce. If you like your omelettes soft, fold the egg over the apple pieces and immediately roll the omelette out onto a warm plate. If you prefer a firmer omelette, fold the egg over and allow it to cook for about half a minute longer before sliding it onto the plate. Either way, top the omelette with a generous helping of the sauce, and keep warm while you repeat the process with the remaining omelette and the rest of the sauce. Serve at once.

APPLES FOR A PASTRY CART

The most elegant pastry cart can be filled with these impressive tarts, one luxurious pie and a Scandinavian-style cake.

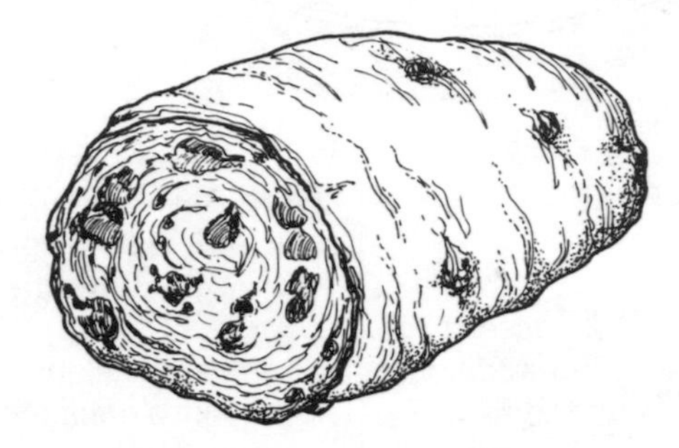

PEASANT GIRL IN A VEIL

I was introduced to this apple cake at a Danish settlement in White City, Florida, where it was displayed, proudly swathed in its "veil" of whipped cream. Since then, I've tasted many variations of this fancifully named dessert—and enjoyed them all. Good fresh pumpernickel or rye breadcrumbs are essential, and you can prepare them while the hot apples are cooling.

Serves 6-8

2 cups water
1 cup sugar
4 tart apples, peeled, cored, and sliced
½ unpeeled lemon, sliced
8 tablespoons butter
2 cups fresh pumpernickel or dark rye breadcrumbs
½ cup heavy cream
1 tablespoon sugar

Combine the water and sugar in a saucepan and stir over moderate heat until the sugar has dissolved. Bring to a boil and add the apples and lemon slices. Cook, uncovered, stirring occasionally, until the apples are tender—about 15 minutes for firm tart apples. Remove from the heat and allow to cool. Remove the lemon slices.

While the apples are cooling, line a dessert bowl or a mold with crisscrossed strips of wax paper. (This will make it easier to unmold the dessert later on.)

Heat the butter in a large skillet. Add the breadcrumbs and cook over moderate heat, stirring constantly, until they are well coated with butter. Layer the crumbs alternately with the apples and their syrup into the lined bowl or mold, ending with a layer of crumbs. Refrigerate for several hours or overnight.

When you are ready to serve,

whip the cream until it starts to thicken, then add the tablespoon of sugar and continue to whip until soft peaks form. Unmold the dessert, remove the wax paper, and spoon the whipped cream over the top of the mold, allowing some to run down the sides. (Or, if you prefer, you can leave the dessert in the bowl and simply spread the whipped cream over the top. In this case, or course, omit the wax paper!)

APPLE SLICES

An old-time treat, apple pie in the square is cut in thin slivers for snacks, desserts or lunchboxes.

Serves 6 generously
Preheat the oven to 375 degrees

Pastry:
1 cup flour
½ teaspoon salt
2 tablespoons butter
2 tablespoons lard or vegetable shortening
1 egg yolk
¼ cup water

Filling:
¼ cup chopped pecans or walnuts
1½ pounds tart apples
1 teaspoon lemon juice
½ cup sugar
1 tablespoon cornstarch
½ teaspoon cinnamon

Mix together the flour and salt. Cut in the butter and the shortening with 2 knives or with a pastry blender. Add the egg yolk and the water and mix lightly with a fork. Pull the mixture together in a ball and divide it into 2 parts. Roll out one part on a pastry cloth into a square to fit and 8-inch square baking pan. Fit the pastry into the pan, being careful not to stretch it.

Sprinkle the chopped nuts over the pastry in the pan. Peel, core and cut the apples into cubes. Toss them with the lemon juice, sugar, cornstarch and cinnamon. Spread the apple filling over the pastry in the pan.

Roll out the remaining pastry into an 8-inch square and fit it over the filling, trimming or tucking in the edges. Slit the pastry in several places to allow steam to escape. Bake on the lower shelf of the oven until the crust is browned and the apples are tender, approximately 50 to 55 minutes. Serve warm or at room temperature.

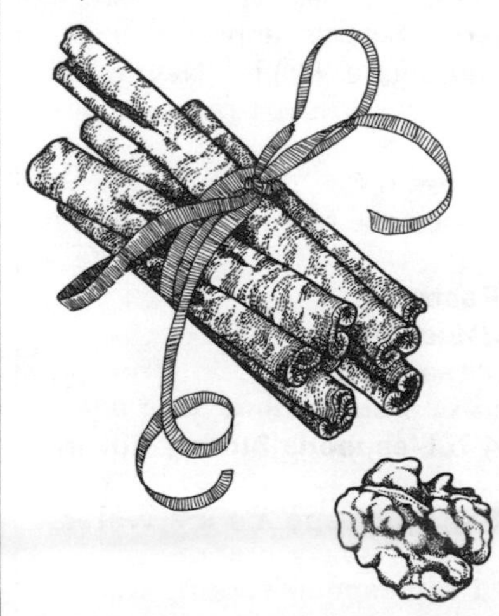

SPIRITED APPLE PIE

Without the spirits, this is a glorious conventional apple pie; made with spirits, each wedge has a rich sauce that blends into the whipped cream served with the pie. It deserves the tartest, most flavorful apples you can find, such as Pippins, Newtowns, Northern Spys or Granny Smiths.

Serves 6-8
Preheat the oven to 425 degrees

Pastry:
2½ cups flour
1 teaspoon salt
⅔ cup shortening
4 tablespoons butter, cut in slices
8-10 tablespoons ice water

Filling:
6 cups thinly sliced tart apples
1 teaspoon cinnamon
¾ cup sugar
1 tablespoon flour
1 tablespoon freshly squeezed lemon juice (if apples are sweet)
⅓-½ cup Calvados, applejack or bourbon, if using spirits; if not, substitute ¼ cup apple juice

To prepare the pastry, combine the flour and salt and cut in the shortening with a pastry blender or 2 knives until the mixture is flaky. Cut in the butter until the mixture looks like coarse crumbs. Add 3 or 4 tablespoons of the ice water and mix with a fork. Add

the remaining water, using just enough to form a dough that clings. Shape the dough into a ball, wrap it in wax paper and chill for at least 30 minutes. Roll out half the pastry into an 11- or 12-inch round. Fit it gently into a deep 9-inch pie plate, letting the edges fall over the rim of the plate. Do not trim. Chill the remaining dough.

To prepare the filling, combine the apples, cinnamon, nutmeg, sugar and flour in a bowl. Toss to mix well and to draw the juices from the apples. If the apples are sweet, add 1 tablespoon of lemon juice and toss. Turn the filling into the pie shell.

Roll out the remaining pastry into an 11-inch round. Fit it loosely over the filling and pull the center to a peak. Fold the bottom layer of pastry over the edge of the top layer, and flute the edge to form an upright rim. Carefully cut a hole in the peak you have made in the center of the pie and fit into it a small funnel, a cake-decorating tip with a large opening, or a tube shaped from heavy-duty aluminum foil.

Place a sheet of foil loosely on the oven floor to catch any drips. Bake the pie on the lowest rack for 10 minutes, then reduce the heat to 350 degrees. Carefully pour ¼ cup of the Calvados or 2 tablespoons apple juice into the funnel so that it drizzles gradually into the filling. Bake for 30 to 40 minutes longer, until the crust is golden and the apples are tender.

While the pie is baking, occasionally pour in a tablespoon or two of Calvados or apple juice. If the sauce starts to bubble over onto the foil shield, stop adding liquid. Serve the pie warm with whipped cream or ice cream, spooning the sauce in the filling onto each wedge.

TARTE TATIN

Two sisters named Tatin invented this world-famous tart at their inn on the Loire River in France. Like many European ranges, theirs had no oven, so the tart was baked on the grill. This adaptation is for an American oven, but it solves the problems of caramelizing the apples for the richest flavor.

Serves 6-8
Preheat the oven to 400 degrees

Pastry:
1 cup flour
¼ teaspoon salt
4 tablespoons cold butter, cut in thin slices
2 tablespoons shortening
¼-⅓ cup ice water

Filling:
3 tablespoons butter
¼ cup sugar
4 apples (1¼ pounds), peeled, cored and sliced
¼-⅓ cup sugar
1 teaspoon vanilla

To prepare the pastry, combine the flour and salt in a bowl or food processor fitted with a steel blade. Add the butter and blend it in with a pastry blender or with the pulse action of the food processor to form coarse flakes. Add the shortening and blend or process the mixture until it is crumbly. Add 3 tablespoons of the water and blend it in with a fork or using short pulses of the processor until the pastry clings together in a ball, adding more water as needed. Wrap the dough in wax paper and chill it for 2 hours or longer, until it is firm enough to roll.

Heat the butter in a heavy 9-inch skillet (preferably black iron or other dark material) over moderate heat. Add the 1/4 cup sugar, stirring it in well, and cook until it is a pale caramel color. Remove from the heat. Combine the apples with 1/4 to 1/3 cup of sugar, depending on their sweetness. Add the vanilla and mix well. If desired, arrange some apples in a pattern in the butter mixture in the skillet. Turn the remaining apple filling into the skillet and level it roughly.

Roll out the pastry between 2 sheets of lightly floured wax paper into a 12-inch circle. Carefully drape the pastry over the apples, pushing the edges down around the apples. Bake on the lowest rack of the oven for 30 minutes. If the crust is not browning move the tart to the highest rack. Continue to bake until the crust is lightly browned and the apples are tender, approximately 15 to 20 minutes longer. Remove the tart from the oven, let it stand for 10 minutes and then invert it onto a serving plate. If the apples slip, push them into place with a spatula.

Serve hot, warm or cold with whipped cream.

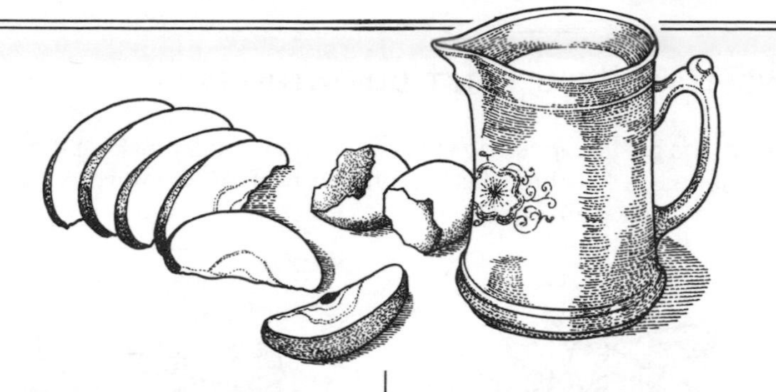

APPLE CREAM TART

Served warm or cold, this tart is handsome enough to be the centerpiece of a dessert buffet.

Serves 6-8
Preheat the oven to 450 degrees

Crust:
1¼ cups flour
¼ teaspoon salt
8 tablespoons cold butter, cut in thin slices
1 egg yolk
About 2 tablespoons cold water

2 apples (Golden Delicious, Granny Smith or other apple that holds its shape)
2 eggs
½ cup sugar
3 tablespoons flour
½ cup heavy cream
1½ teaspoons lemon juice
2 teaspoons sugar

Combine the flour and salt in a bowl or food processor fitted with a steel blade. Cut the butter in with a pastry blender or with a few seconds of processor action, until the mixture forms coarse flakes. Add the egg yolk and water and work the mixture with a fork or in the processor just until the dough clings together. Shape it into a ball and, if time allows, chill for 30 minutes.

Roll out the dough on a floured pastry cloth, fit it into a 9-inch quiche pan with a removable bottom and bake for 8 to 10 minutes, just until it is barely colored. Cool slightly. Reduce the oven temperature to 350 degrees.

Peel and core the apples, cut them into quarters and slice them thinly to form wedge-shaped slices. Fan out the slices of each apple quarter from the center to the rim of the pastry shell to form a pattern.

Beat the eggs thoroughly and beat in the sugar, flour, cream and lemon juice. Place the tart on the center rack of the oven and carefully pour the filling around the apple slices. Sprinkle with 2 teaspoons of sugar. Bake at 350 degrees for 40 to 50 minutes, until the apples are tender and the filling is firm.

MISCELLANY YOU CAN'T DO WITHOUT

Some of the best recipes don't fit neat chapter titles, and here they are; a few soups, a fine breakfast or brunch muffin, snack spreads and relishes to serve with meats.

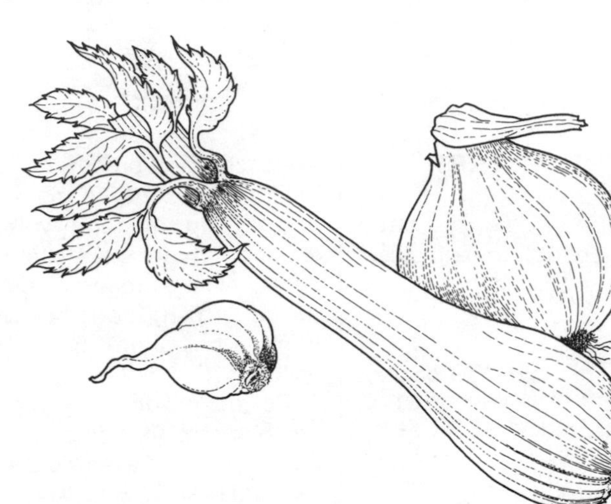

ORIENTAL PEPPER POT

This adaptation of an Indian soup shows off leftover chicken or turkey in fine style. It is even worth cooking the chicken for a freshly made soup.

Serves 4

2 tablespoons butter
1 rib celery, chopped
1 small onion, chopped
2 cloves garlic, minced
1 Cortland or other firm tart apple, peeled, cored and cubed
¾-1 cup diced cooked chicken or turkey
2 teaspoons curry powder
2 cups chicken broth
Salt
Freshly ground black pepper
Hot cooked rice (optional)

Heat the butter in a large saucepan. Add the celery and onion. Cook until the onion is tender but not browned. Add the garlic and apple and cook, stirring gently, until the apple cubes are coated with butter. Add the chicken and curry powder. Mix well and cook for approximately 30 seconds to allow the curry flavor to permeate the other ingredients. Add the chicken broth, bring to a boil, cover and simmer for 5 to 10 minutes. Add salt and pepper to taste.

Serve over hot rice in large soup plates.

APPLE-FRUIT SOUP

Choose full-flavored apples such as Greenings, Gravensteins or Northern Spys for this. The soup may be served hot or cold.

Serves 6-8

1 pound (1½ cups) mixed dried fruit
2½ quarts water
1½ pounds (5 small) tart, full-flavored apples
2 2-inch sticks cinnamon
½ lemon with rind
¼ cup sugar
Salt to taste
¼ cup cornstarch mixed with ½ cup water
Sour cream or ricotta cheese

Cook the dried fruit in 1 quart of the water until tender. Save a few attractive pieces for decoration, if desired.

Core and cut the apples into eighths. Combine the apples, 1½ quarts of water, the cinnamon and the half lemon in another large saucepan. Bring to a boil and simmer until the apples are very tender, 20 to 25 minutes. Discard the cinnamon and lemon. Puree both the dried fruit and the apple mixtures in a food mill, blender or food processor.

Return the soup to the saucepan and bring it to a boil, once more. Stir in the sugar, salt to taste and the cornstarch mixture. Cook and stir until the soup is smooth and slightly thickened, about 2 minutes. Serve hot with a spoonful of sour cream or ricotta in each bowlful, or chill it first and then serve, decorated with fruit.

APPLE-CAULIFLOWER SOUP

Broccoli may be combined with or used in place of cauliflower in this recipe, if desired.

Serves 6-8

1 tablespoon butter
1 apple, peeled and chopped
1 onion, chopped
1 pound cauliflower or broccoli, or a combination
⅛ teaspoon nutmeg
2 cups chicken or beef broth
Salt
Freshly ground black pepper
1 cup milk or light cream
Garnish: Red-skinned apple slices; sliced cauliflower or broccoli florets

Heat the butter in a large kettle. Add the chopped apple and onion and sauté them until the onion is tender but not browned. Add the cauliflower, nutmeg, broth and salt and pepper to taste. Cover and simmer until the cauliflower is tender, 18 to 20 minutes. Puree the mixture in a food mill, blender or food processor. Reheat it, adding the milk, but do not allow it to boil. Ladle the soup into warm bowls and garnish each serving with a slice of apple and vegetable.

DANISH APPLE SOUP

Firm, tart apples such as Rome Beauties, Grimes Golden, Staymans and late-season Granny Smiths thicken this soup sufficiently so that it usually needs no cornstarch. It may be served hot or cold as a first course or a dessert.

Serves 6

2 pounds (6-8) apples
2 quarts water
1 cinnamon stick, broken
Peel of 1 lemon, cut in a spiral
2-4 tablespoons sugar
2-4 tablespoons cornstarch (optional)
Water for mixing cornstarch
Toasted French bread

Core and quarter the apples, but do not peel them. Place them in a large saucepan with the water, cinnamon stick and lemon peel. Cover and simmer until the apples are very soft. Remove the cinnamon stick and lemon peel. Force the apples and liquid through a food mill or strainer. Return the mixture to the saucepan, add the sugar and cook, stirring, until the sugar has dissolved.

If a thicker soup is desired, blend the cornstarch with enough water to make a smooth paste. Stir the paste into the soup and cook, stirring, until the soup is smooth and has thickened. Serve hot or cold with toast on the side or in each soup plate. The soup can be garnished with whipped cream or sour cream sprinkled with cinnamon.

SPICED APPLE-BRAN MUFFINS

Makes 12 medium-sized muffins
Preheat the oven to 400 degrees

1 cup whole bran cereal
1¼ cups milk
1 cup finely chopped peeled tart apple
1¼ cups flour
1 tablespoon baking powder
1½ teaspoons ginger or cardamom
¼ teaspoon salt

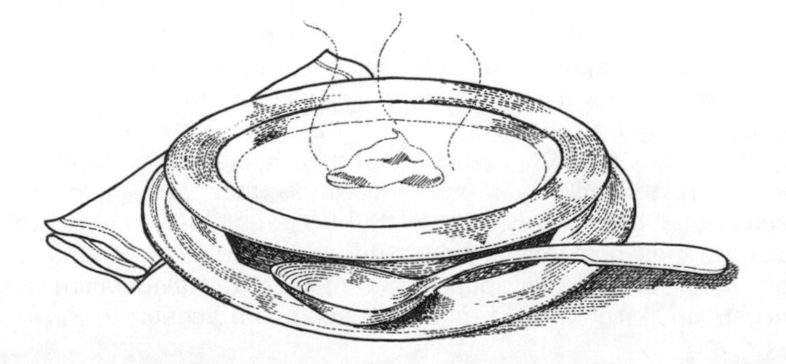

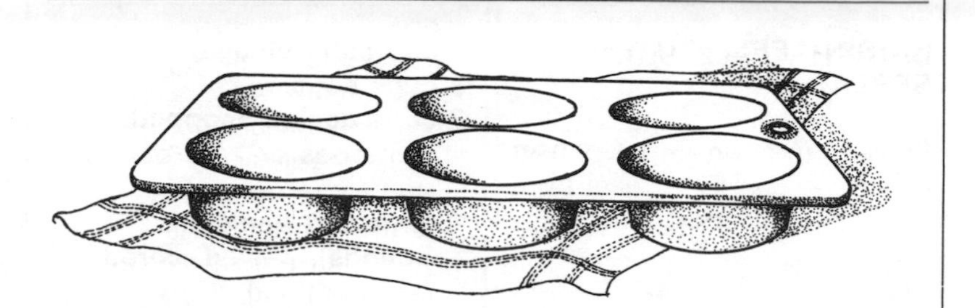

2 tablespoons sugar
1 egg, slightly beaten
¼ cup oil

Combine the bran cereal with the milk in a medium-sized bowl. Let stand until the cereal is softened and the milk is absorbed, about 10 minutes. Add the chopped apple and mix well. Stir in the flour, baking powder spice, salt and sugar. Add the egg and oil and stir until well mixed.

Spoon the batter into a well-greased or paper-cup-lined muffin tin. Bake for 25 minutes or until puffed and lightly browned, and a toothpick inserted into the center of a muffin comes out clean. Serve hot with butter.

APPLE TRIMMINGS JELLY

Tart apples of late summer are the most reliable for jelly, but this novelty is fun anytime. If the apples have lost their pectin or acid to old age, you still have a flavorful syrup for pancakes or a sweetener for baked apples and puddings. This homemade version of common apple jelly is surprisingly good!

Makes about 2 pints

Peels, cores and seeds from 6-8 apples
3 cups water, approximately
Sugar

Pack the apple trimmings lightly into a large saucepan and add water to not quite cover. Cover the saucepan and simmer for 20 minutes, until the juice is lightly colored and slightly thickened by the natural pectin.

Strain the juice through a clean cotton towel or several layers of cheesecloth in a colander over a saucepan or 1-quart measure. Place the juice and an equal amount of sugar in a saucepan. Stir over high heat until the sugar has dissolved. Bring to a boil, lower the heat, but maintain a rolling boil until the syrup slides together in one thick drop to fall from the testing spoon. Immediately pour the syrup into clean hot jars. Cover and refrigerate.

To store the jelly in a cupboard, sterilize the jars and all equipment such as funnels, lifters and jar lids before filling the jars. Seal the jelly with paraffin and cover the jars tightly.

RAISIN-APPLE-NUT SPREAD

Spread this on whole-wheat bread and cut it in fingers for a lunchbox or snack.

Makes about 1½ cups

¾ cup raisins
1 teaspoon sugar (to prevent sticky blender or processor blades)
¾ cup walnuts
2 small apples, peeled, cored and sliced
1 tablespoon mayonnaise

Combine the raisins with the sugar in a blender or food processor. Process until the raisins are chopped finely. Add the walnuts, a few at a time, and continue to process until well mixed. Add the apples, a few pieces at a time, and process until a thick paste is formed. (If a blender or processor is unavailable, use a food mill.) Turn the spread into a small bowl and work in the mayonnaise, adding more if needed to moisten. Serve this spread on thinly sliced bread or on crackers.

HOT APPLE CHUTNEY

This chutney has enough fire to suit the hardiest chili buffs. Use half as much chili for a milder condiment.

Fills 4 ½-pint jars

1 cup cider vinegar
3 cups sugar
2 cups peeled chopped tomatoes or 14½-ounce can tomatoes
6 large tart apples (2 pounds), peeled, cored and chopped
1 teaspoon salt
1 tablespoon ground ginger or 2 tablespoons minced ginger root
½ cup chopped chilies (fresh, canned or pickled hot cherry peppers)
1 large onion, chopped
2 large cloves garlic, chopped
1 cup raisins

Combine the vinegar with the sugar in a large stainless steel or enamelware saucepan. Bring to a boil, stirring, until the sugar has dissolved. Simmer until the mixture is syrupy, about 5 minutes.

Add the tomatoes, apples, salt, ginger, chilies, onion, garlic and raisins. Simmer, uncovered, until the mixture has thickened so that a spoon drawn through the center leaves a track, about 20 to 30 minutes. Stir often while cooking, as chutney scorches easily.

When done, spoon the chutney into hot jars, cover and refrigerate. For cupboard storage, seal in canning jars as manufacturer directs, and process in a boiling-water bath for 10 minutes for 1/2 pints. Serve the chutney with curries, and with cold or roast meats.

APPLE-APRICOT CONSERVE

This is a colorful relish for cold meats and makes a luxurious spread for hot biscuits or rolls.

Fills 4 ½-pint jars

½ pound (¾ cup) dried apricots
2 cups hot water
1 cup sugar
1½ pounds tart apples, peeled and sliced
½ cup raisins
2 tablespoons cider vinegar
½ cup coarsely chopped walnuts

Combine the apricots with the hot water in a saucepan and let stand for 30 minutes to 1 hour. Then cook the apricots until they are tender, stirring occasionally, and adding more water, if needed, to prevent burning. (However, the juice should be thick when the apricots have finished cooking.)

Stir in the sugar, apples and raisins. Cover and simmer until the apples are tender. Stir in the vinegar and walnuts. Ladle the mixture into clean hot jars. Cover and refrigerate, or seal the jars as manufacturer directs and process in a boiling-water bath for 10 minutes.

APRICOT-APPLE JAM

Serve this jam in your prettiest jam jar as a spread for toast or as a relish for meats.

Makes about 1½ pints

½ pound (about ¾ cup) dried apricots
1½ cups water
2 apples, peeled, cored and chopped
½ cup Calvados or applejack
1 cup sugar

Combine the apricots with the water in a stainless steel or enamelware pan. Bring to a boil, turn the heat low and simmer until the apricots are tender. Add the apples, Calvados and sugar. Mix well, cover and cook, stirring occasionally, until the mixture is very tender and almost smooth. If it is too moist, cook rapidly over high heat, stirring constantly, until the mixture has thickened. Turn the jam into hot clean jars. Cover and cool. Refrigerate for up to 6 weeks. For longer storage, seal and process as above.

FROM IRENA CHALMERS COOKBOOKS, INC.

BOOKS BY COOKS

America's Best Recipes
An Apple a Day
Appetizers
Beautiful Soup
A Book of Graces (table blessings for the family)
Casseroles
Cheesecakes
Chinese Appetizers
Cookies and Candies (for Christmas and all year long)
Clay Cookery
Cooking with Flowers
Cooking with Steamers
Dinner in Half an Hour
Edible Table Decorations
Fabulous Fruitcakes
Foods of Greece
Gifts from the Christmas Kitchen
Ice Cream
Mountains of Chocolate
Napkin Folds
A Pocketful of Pies
Sauces Made While the Pasta Cooks
Sushi and Sashimi and Soup and Tempura
Tacos, Tortillas and Tostados
Trim a Treat (Christmas decorations you can eat)
Vodka n' Vittles
Wine and Cheese
Wok Cooking

THE INTERNATIONAL ASSOCIATION OF COOKING SCHOOLS COOKBOOK

THE MARVELOUS MACADAMIA NUT

THE GREAT AMERICAN COOKING SCHOOLS

American Food & California Wine
Bountiful Bread: Basics to Brioches
Christmas Feasts from History
Cooking from a Country Kitchen
Cooking of the South
Dim Sum & Chinese One-Dish Meals
Fair Game: A Hunter's Cookbook
Fine Fresh Food—Fast
Fresh Garden Vegetables
Ice Cream & Ices
Microwave Cooking: Meals in Minutes
Old-Fashioned Desserts
Omelettes & Soufflés
Pasta! Cooking It, Loving It
Quiche & Pâté
Romantic & Classic Cakes
Soups & Salads
Successful Parties: Simple & Elegant